# ZOO ANIMAL
## MYSTERIES

# A Saltwater Stumper

by Martha E. H. Rustad

**Consulting Editor:** Gail Saunders-Smith, PhD

**Consultant:** Jackie Gai, DVM
Zoo and Exotic Animal Consultant

CAPSTONE PRESS
a capstone imprint

Pebble Plus is published by Capstone Press,
151 Good Counsel Drive, P.O. Box 669, Mankato, Minnesota 56002.
www.capstonepub.com

032010
005740CGF10

 Books published by Capstone Press are manufactured with paper
containing at least 10 percent post-consumer waste.

*Library of Congress Cataloging-in-Publication Data*
Rustad, Martha E. H. (Martha Elizabeth Hillman), 1975–
   A saltwater stumper : a zoo animal mystery / by Martha E.H. Rustad.
      p. cm.—(Pebble plus. Zoo animal mysteries)
   Includes bibliographical references and index.
   Summary: "Simple text and full-color photographs present a mystery zoo animal, one feature at a time, until its identity is
revealed"—Provided by publisher.
   ISBN 978-1-4296-4496-9 (library binding)
   1. Anemonefishes—Juvenile literature. I. Title. II. Series.
   QL638.P77R87 2011
   597'.72—dc22                                            2010001350

**Editorial Credits**
Jenny Marks, editor; Heidi Thompson, designer; Svetlana Zhurkin, media researcher; Eric Manske, production specialist

**Photo Credits**
Alamy/Jesse Cancelmo, 16–17
Capstone Studio/Karon Dubke, 15
Getty Images/Photolibrary/Paulo De Oliveira, 10–11
iStockphoto/Brandon Laufenberg, cover; Jodi Jacobson, 20–21
Photolibrary/JW.Alker, 13
Shutterstock/cbpix, 19; John A. Anderson, 6–7; Martin Valigursky, 4–5
Visuals Unlimited/Reinhard Dirscherl, 9

Note to Parents and Teachers

The Mystery Zoo Animals series supports national science standards related to life science. This
book describes and illustrates clown fish. The images support early readers in understanding
the text. The repetition of words and phrases helps early readers learn new words. This book
also introduces early readers to subject-specific vocabulary words, which are defined in the
Glossary section. Early readers may need assistance to read some words and to use the Table of
Contents, Glossary, Read More, Internet Sites, and Index sections of the book.

# Table of Contents

# It's a Mystery

This book is full of clues
about a mystery zoo animal.
And the animal is me!
Can you guess what I am?

Here's your first clue:
In the wild, I live in warm,
shallow water in the Pacific
and Indian Oceans.

North
America

Europe

Asia

Africa

South
America

Australia

Antarctica

Where I Live

5

My home is a coral reef.

Reefs are crowded with life.

They have the perfect

hiding spot, just for me.

But that clue comes later!

# My Life and Kids

My mate builds a nest near
our hiding place. Hundreds of
orange eggs sit in our nest.
My mate keeps our eggs safe
from predators.

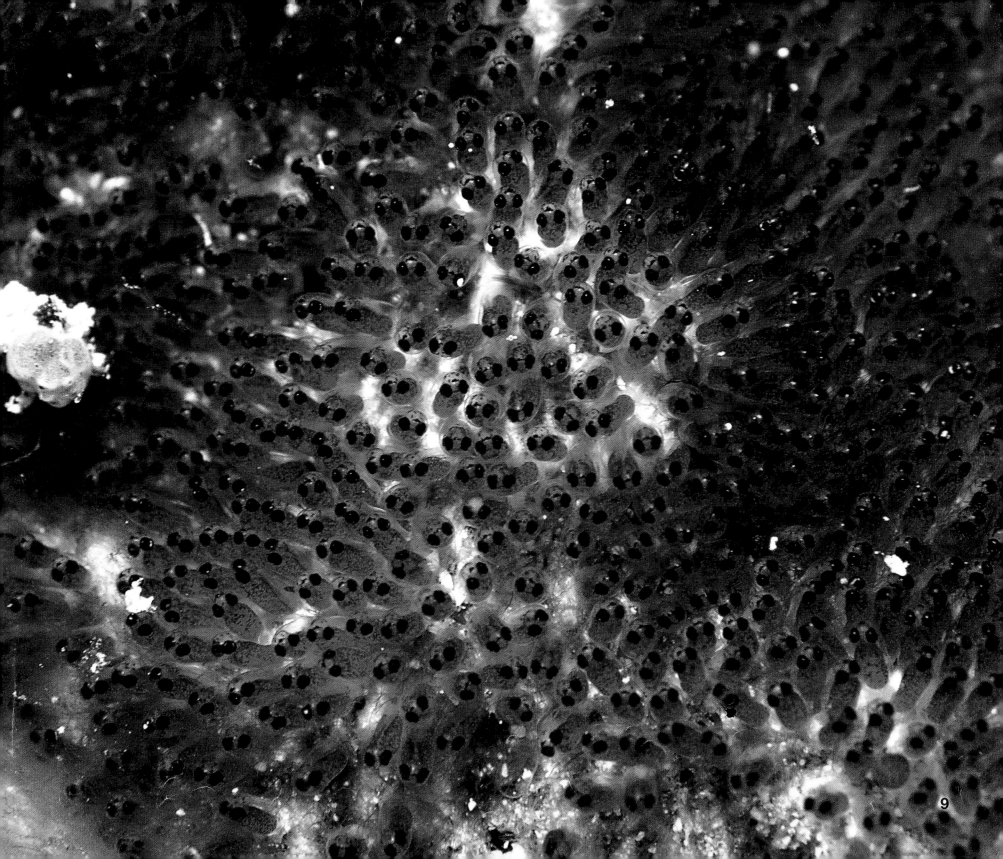
9

In four or five days,

our babies hatch.

They float away to find

their own hiding places.

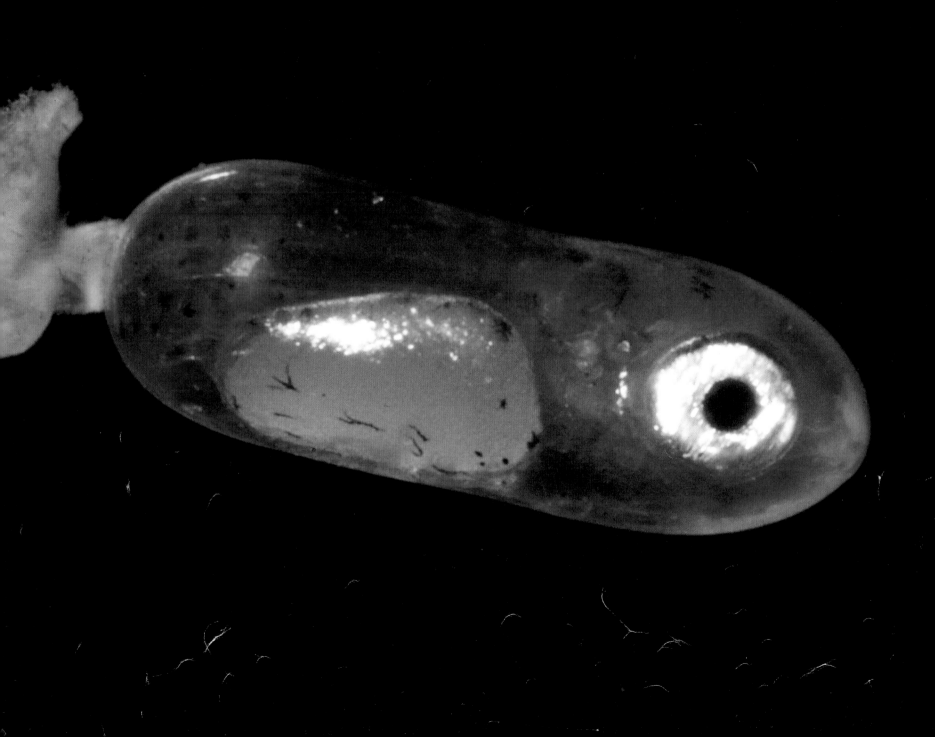

# Body Parts

My fins move me through

warm ocean waters.

Side fins help me steer.

My top fin keeps me

from flipping upside down.

My body is covered

with bright scales.

A coat of slime

protects my body

from creatures that sting.

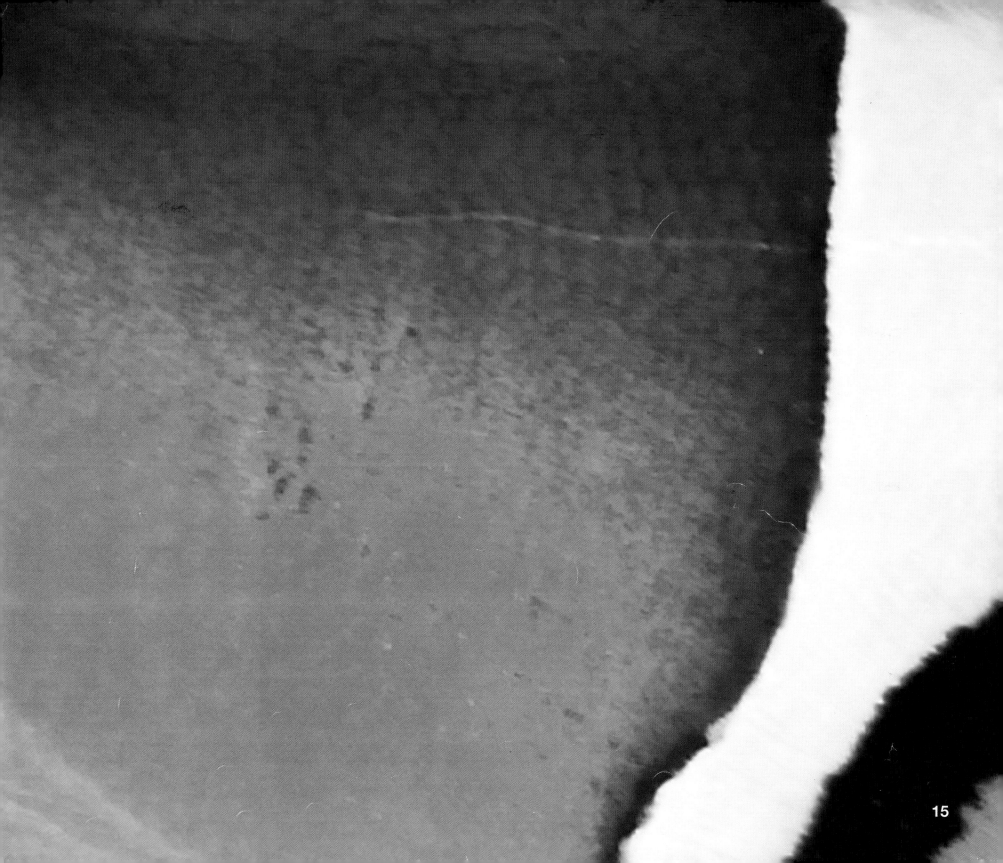

15

I can safely snuggle in

the arms of my sea anemone.

Sea anemones sting anything

that swims nearby.

But the stings don't hurt me.

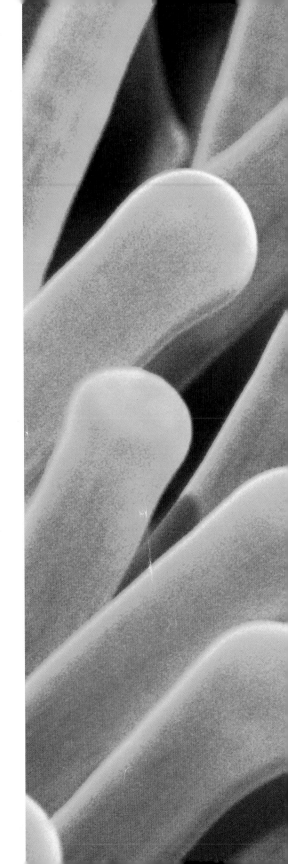

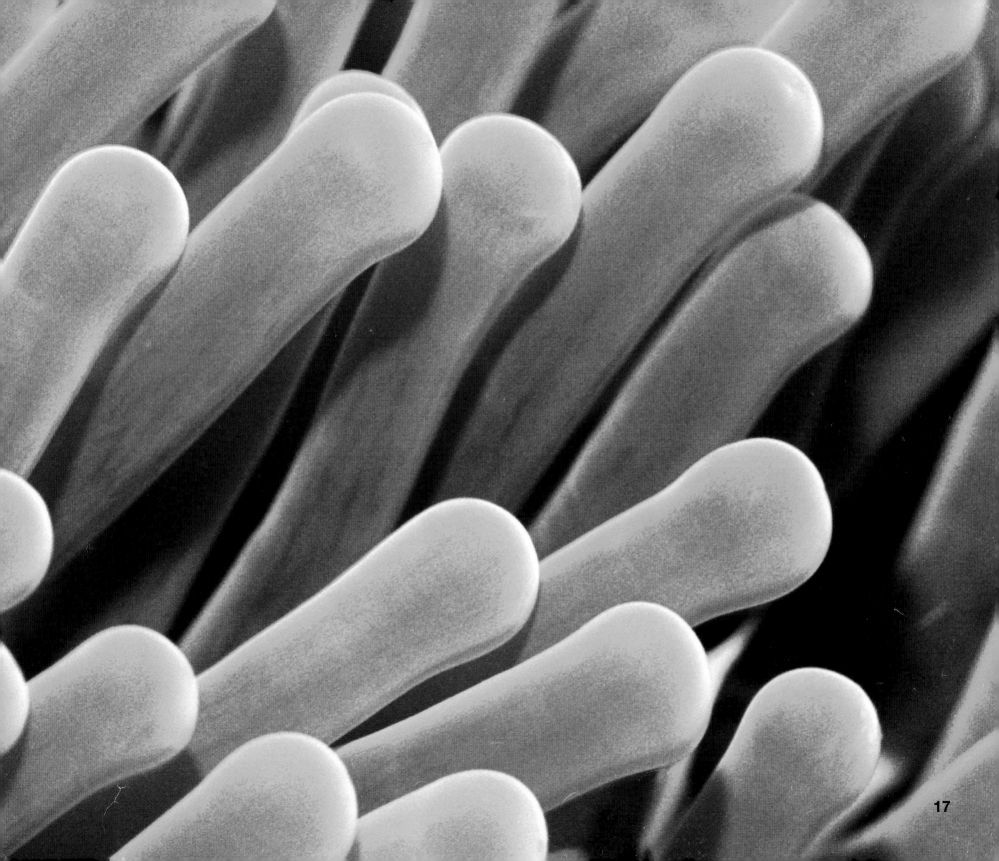

17

Orange, black, and white

stripes cover my body.

Bright colors tell predators

to stay away.


Have you guessed what I am?

19

# Mystery Solved!

I'm a clown fish!

This zoo mystery is solved.

# Glossary

coral reef—a type of land made up of the hardened skeletons of corals; corals are small, colorful sea creatures

hatch—to break out of an egg

mate—the male or female partner of a pair of animals

predator—an animal that hunts other animals for food

scale—one of the small, thin plates that covers the bodies of fish

sea anemone—a sea animal with a tube-shaped body and many tentacles

slime—a soft, slippery substance

sting—to hurt with a poisoned tip; sea anemones can sting prey with their tentacles

# Read More

**Sexton, Colleen A.** *Clown Fish.* Oceans Alive. Minneapolis: Bellwether Media, 2007.

**Stille, Darlene R.** *I Am a Fish: The Life of a Clown Fish.* I Live in the Ocean. Minneapolis: Picture Window Books, 2005.

**Taylor, Leighton R.** *Anemone Fish.* Early Bird Nature Books. Minneapolis: Lerner, 2007.

# Internet Sites

FactHound offers a safe, fun way to find Internet sites related to this book. All of the sites on FactHound have been researched by our staff.

Here's all you do:

Visit *www.facthound.com*

Type in this code: 9781429644969

# Index

Word Count: 202
Grade: 1
Early-Intervention Level: 15